imaginary

TALL TALE TELLING

**24 fun games for making
and telling incredible stories**

Rob Parkinson

Book 1 in the series "Natural Storytelling"
Published by Imaginary Journeys
27 London Road, Tonbridge, Kent TN10 3AB UK
Tel/fax +44 (0) 1732 362356
E-mail: info@imaginaryjourneys.co.uk

www.imaginaryjourneys.co.uk

All rights reserved. No part of this publication may be reproduced, stored in a retrieval system, transmitted or used in any form or by any means, electronic, mechanical, photocopying, recording or otherwise without the prior permission of the copyright holder.

First published October 2004
© Rob Parkinson 2004

ISBN – 0-9549001-0-5

TALL TALE TELLING

Contents

	Introduction	p.3
1.	Fantastic Fibs	p.6
2.	Pass it On	p.8
3.	Wicked Whoppers	p.10
4.	In Your Dreams	p.12
5.	Whodunnit	p.14
6.	Future Fantasies	p.16
7.	Hazards & Challenges	p.18
8.	The House that Daisy Built	p.20
9.	The One that Got Away	p.22
10.	A Funny Thing Happened	p.24
11.	Being Joe Bloggs	p.26
12.	Peculiar People	p.28
13.	Excellent Excuses	p.30
14.	Rum Rumours	p.32
15.	Smoke Without Fire	p.34
16.	Springboards	p.36
17.	Bragging	p.38
18.	My friend Boogle	p.40
19.	Rapid Reversals	p.42
20.	Challenging Changes	p.44
21.	Time Changes	p.46
22.	I Went to the Pictures Tomorrow	p.48
23.	Magic Islands & Strange Planets	p.50
24.	News for the Emperor	p.52

INTRODUCTION

I'm only telling you lies so that you can get to the truth.
(Traditional storyteller's paradox)

The games in this collection have come out of hundreds of practical workshops for children, teenagers and adults I've run as a professional teller of tales over the last twenty years. Some of them go back further to a spell in teaching I did more than thirty years ago.

The booklet is the first of a series of four, each of which explores different aspects of story making and telling through lively and imaginative game techniques. Most of these games are original, though a few are adaptations of more widely known games. Some appeared in a series I did for the Society for Storytelling's magazine/newsletter, *Storylines* in the 'nineties whilst brief selections have appeared elsewhere. I've often been asked for more of them, hence these publications, which are intended for use by all kinds of people who want to explore and develop natural capacities with story, including teachers and parents, therapists, trainers and of course storytellers.

Together, the four booklets in the series can form a coherent approach to developing what I'm calling 'the natural storyteller' – the combination of imaginative, verbal and other skills we use in all sorts of activities apart from things we designate as actual story telling, reading and making. This is an idea I explore at much greater length in a book for Human Givens publishing entitled *Storying for Solutions*, scheduled for publication during 2005.

Tall Tale Telling uses, in a positive and constructive way, a natural skill we have which is too often expressed only in lying, excuse making and gossip. All good story teaching (and maybe all good teaching) should start from what we do naturally. This doesn't have to mean encouraging anyone to habitually tell fibs, though the feeling of slight wickedness is a good motivator for many children. As pointed out elsewhere in the notes, the games are paradoxically much more likely to encourage truth spotting than lying, because they encourage use of the critical faculties in partnership with fantasy.

The presentation of some of the games might make them seem most appropriate to primary and younger secondary age children, though the techniques have been used highly effectively with older teenagers and adults as well. It's often a question of simply adapting the label and adjusting the kind of fantasy to suit. Each game is accompanied by three kinds of notes:-

General note: In this category are included various practical tips on taking the game further, on practical procedures and alternatives as well as notes on connections with other kinds of story/ work around stories and points of incidental interest. With any game, it should be possible to re-invent it many times over in different forms; the hints in this section sometimes suggest this, though experiment is probably the better teacher.

Story Skills: Points here cover ideas specifically about story and language coming out of each game. Space (perhaps fortunately) does not allow the extensive essays I could offer here, but anyone with an imaginative grasp of this subject will see the many possibilities.

Interesting: In this category, I've briefly flagged up some alternative uses of the games in areas like emotional intelligence teaching, moral education, therapy and counselling etc. Whilst this can at first seem incongruous in a book of imaginative techniques, this is an important aspect of these techniques I've explored at length in my own work in recent times and deserves at least a suggestion or two. Intelligent teaching of and working with stories takes account of the fact that story (even wild, unbridled fantasy story and pure fib) always connects with a sense of meaning at some level.

But the games are meant to be first of all fun – to be to anyone playing them just that; I'd be the last to want to make them into po-faced 'serious exercises'. Learning should be fun, a fact too often forgotten by pompous and fundamentally ignorant politicians and pundits – not just to 'sugar the pill', but because it is far more effective to use natural enjoyment and absorption, allowing learning to take place on many levels simultaneously. In my view at least, in recent years far too many horses have been ostentatiously led to far too much water without anyone apparently noticing that not much real drinking has been going on. If we tickled them a bit more, they might just get thirsty.

Rob Parkinson September 2004

1.
FANTASTIC FIBS

(The Basic Tall Tale Telling Game a.k.a. Tall Stories)
Large & small groups/pairs and trios

One person is the storyteller. S/he claims to have done or seen (etc.) something unbelievable. This could be in the realms of pure fantasy (riding a magic carpet, seeing a dragon, shape shifting etc.) or it could be just beyond the mundane (becoming a celeb for a day, playing for a major football club, winning a million etc.). Then again, it could be simply absurd and improbable (growing an extra arm, bouncing down the main road on bed springs, riding a jet-propelled toilet etc). The type of fib talked about and illustrated can be varied to suit age etc. It can be presented in a sentence or two or at greater length.

The partner or other group members ask questions designed to test the truth of the tale. These can be limited to a set number initially (say 5 or 7) or perhaps within a set time (say 2 to 5 minutes). No one is allowed to challenge the truth of the tale directly ("That couldn't happen!" "It's impossible…" etc.) neither can the storyteller be asked whether it is a fib ("Are you lying? Is that true?" etc.). Questions ask for detail and explanation. (If you rode a magic carpet, you'd have a good idea of how it felt, maybe roughly how you controlled it, what colour and size it was, how you came to be on it etc.) As long as the storyteller can answer, the story is true and s/he is winning.

Once questions are finished, the 'story' can be reviewed and retold using as many of the details emerging from the questioning as can be remembered. A good way to do this is through the next game, *Pass it On*.

Note: Fantastic Fibs works marvellously with both pairs, threes and both small and large groups across a very broad age range – I've regularly used it with children of all school ages and in workshops with adults. Developments suggested below apply to many of the other games. Fantastic Fibs can also be played with pairs, threes and small groups (as in Game 14 Rum Rumours). My song, Tall Stories on The Wonderful Store CD (IJ101) or tape (ML1001) is useful alongside this game with young children and the lyric is available free from the Imaginary Journeys web site.

Story skills: This game externalises what happens in the fiction making mind. Writers play a version of it with themselves as they write and storytellers do so as they speak. ("This or that could/will happen.... but how does that work? How do I make it real? ".) The 'fantasist' alternates with the 'critic' and the story grows out of the interaction. Participants can later try the game inside their own minds. Stories can be remembered by the teller and developed through repeated telling in Pass it On, exercising storytelling ability in two ways. A further speaking and listening activity is to record the story on tape, CD etc. when it is sufficiently developed. The story can also be written down by the teller.

Interesting: Some teachers and others like to present this game under another title to avoid mixed moral messages. But a) it actually encourages listeners to spot lies and ask intelligent questions and b) it increases awareness of how lying works, which frequently decreases the tendency to tell lies. In the therapeutic use of the game, an individual is encouraged to tell a tall tale which is essentially a fantasy version of the action s/he needs to master and is then asked subtle questions by the mentor/therapist etc., as explained in Storying for Solutions.

2.
PASS IT ON

Large & small groups; pairs; trios

This game is for varied use following any of the Tall Tale Telling games that can be played or developed in pairs or small groups. Once the first game has been tried in a pair or small group, participants change partners or group. In *Fantastic Fibs* played as a pair game for example, each partner now has two stories a) the one they made up themselves and were asked questions about and b) the one their partner made up. In Pass it On, the first thing the storyteller does is to re-tell either a) or b) or both (as directed by the group leader, or as decided by the players). This can be straight telling or it can involve more questioning. The pair can then swap new tall tales and go on to another pair, having now an option of four different tales to pass on.

It's possible to continue further. Pairs can move to groups of four and larger groups, or pairs can go on changing and swapping stories so that a larger and larger number of tales have to be known. Once the larger group/class etc. convenes again, tellers might be challenged to tell as many of the tall tales they heard as possible. Or they might be asked to tell their favourite tale. It is interesting to see how this may have changed since it was invented by another group member.

General Note: Though this can be seen as a technique for developing any of the games rather than a separate game in itself, children especially respond to calling it a separate game. It makes an instant label for a stage after a game which the group may or may not 'play' in a session and it can be varied in all sorts of ways, from those suggested above to well known passing it on games like Chinese Whispers.

Story Skills: Because so much teaching of story in our culture has focused on the written word, there's a feeling that you create a story once and for all in one form. This is quite unlike much of the natural, everyday storytelling we do, where we change and adapt our news or gossip or anecdotes on the hoof. Stories told repeatedly develop and grow, naturally. This game teaches that process, develops social confidence and skill in speaking, listening and remembering.

Interesting: The game shows a lot about how stories and rumours grow and change. Separating fact from fiction (or from spin and hype) is a sadly neglected but actually very vital skill in the contemporary world. It is possible to adapt Pass it On as a game for studying rumour and its various cousins, innuendo, gossip, supposition, suspicion, spin etc.

3.
WICKED WHOPPERS

Large & small groups; pairs

Wicked Whoppers is third person singular tall stories. It works in the same way as Fantastic Fibs, but the storyteller has to tell a tale about someone else not present. This could be a family member or a friend or an acquaintance or it could even be a celebrity of some kind. However, the storyteller must advance good and sufficient reasons for believing it to be true (i.e. they haven't just heard it here and there as a rumour and believed it). The questions from partner or group work in the same way as for the basic Tall Telling Game, with qualifiers as in the explanations below.

(**Theydunnit** is third person plural tall stories and works in the same way, though of course is about they and them.)

———————

Note: Once Fantastic Fibs has been played successfully, it's easy to introduce Wicked Whoppers, simply explaining the slight difference. With children, it's useful to emphasize the ways in which questions might be different, the kinds of flaws one might look for in a tale told about someone else rather than about oneself, what might be 'good and sufficient reasons' etc.

Story Skills: Telling a story about someone else differs from telling a story as the narrator in all sorts of ways, but there are also similarities and cross-over points. This game makes a great platform for teaching this and showing how much it's possible to say about another person in a story – and maybe how one can sometimes disguise supposition etc. in fiction making.

Interesting: People commonly imagine all sorts of things about other people. Many such imaginings go unchallenged and can be very damaging. This game gives a relatively safe situation for examining this, beginning from pure fantasy but progressing subtly, so that questions asked can gently challenge actual limiting perceptions etc.

4.
IN YOUR DREAMS

Pairs usually but also groups large & small

The storyteller describes something s/he 'saw' the partner doing 'in their dreams' (whilst asleep, under a spell, in a trance, under the influence of aliens or mad scientists etc.) The partner has to prove s/he is innocent by looking for very specific flaws in the story. (Not just 'That couldn't be true!" but "If you saw me climbing over the fence, why do I have no cuts or grazes?" "If I was really swimming in my sleep, why was I not wet in the morning?" "How is that you were able to watch me doing that?" etc.). The storyteller has to make her/his fiction as plausible as possible, explaining how the partner was tricked and entranced, the kinds of things they did and the way they were made to forget it all. The partner has (say) seven questions to prove innocence, then it is his/her turn to tell a story about the other person.

In the group version, the storyteller describes something the group were all involved in together, again under some kind of strange influence (mad teacher with a strange truth serum, power mad inspector etc). The group again try to disprove the accusation in seven moves and the storyteller again tries to justify his/her invention.

———————

General Note: This is the second person version of Fantastic Fibs. The mild insult and sense of innocence partners can feel are generally very good motivations for some lively questioning. To avoid partners being too much insulted by the 'story' told about them, it's best to encourage fantastical and unlikely accusations that are obviously absurd rather than things that just might be true. The group leader can always play the part of referee who will rule some 'stories' out of order.

Story Skills: Although it seems that most stories are told in the first or third person, the intention of many tale tellers is to make you feel as if you are the one doing it. And advertising is often more blatant about it, directly using the second person idiom in the narrative. The game can produce a practical understanding of this idiom and lead to further experiments in its use.

Interesting: Future Fantasies can teach empathy and can also rehearse the coping with the outrage many people feel when they are the butt of gossip and rumour. In direct emotional intelligence teaching, the subject matter can move from fantasy to real life situations.

5. WHODUNNIT

Group game with small group/pair/trio tasks

The group invent a mysterious set of 'circs' (happenings, circumstances, objects etc.) and storytellers attempt to explain their connection by telling a story. Suggestions can be taken at random and noted, then finally thinned down to give a manageable number of these – a minimum of three, but the number can be increased with familiarity.

(Example with 5 circs. 1. Black hat with a jagged hole 2. It's beside a purple rocking chair 3. There is an open window banging in the wind 4. There is a fish hanging dangling on a string from the ceiling 5. A loud crash and scream.)

Small groups. pairs, threes etc. can work out a story together at the first stage. Once the game is familiar or with participants already confident, individuals can tell their versions straight away. If appropriate, the group can vote for the best story in different categories – the most sensible, the funniest/silliest/zaniest, most original etc. It's usually best to introduce new 'circs' every so often, rather than hearing too many versions of one set.

General Note: Some people will know riddles and conundrums that work somewhat in this way, for example the one about the lumps of coal, the scarf, the carrot and the hat in the middle of a green field, the connection being a snowman that has now melted. However, these 'clues' are meant to be more open ended and random – you can link them in whatever way and in many different ways. Compare this game with Game 15. Smoke Without Fire.

Story skills: Creating mystery and then gradually solving it is a major ingredient of all sorts of fiction, not just the 'whodunnit' variety this game takes its name from. Linking disparate things to make a story is a very common creative writing technique of which this is an oral variant. The way in which human beings can link things, ideas and images is a part of natural storytelling capacity which needs to be developed and has all kinds of applications beyond story.

Interesting: Leaping to conclusions is all too common and happens in much gossip and news as well as in personal relationships. In teaching emotional intelligence through story, the circumstances etc. set up by the group leader can be made much more emotionally loaded and suggestive. Thus the game can show how facts have much more than one interpretation, especially when combined with some of the questioning techniques used in other games.

6.
FUTURE FANTASIES

Groups & pairs

Before the game starts, the players are all invited to imagine something they really want to do some way into the future (when, for example, they grow up/ are twenty or thirty or sixty-five/ are rich or famous/ brilliant/ powerful/ retired). Subject matter can range anywhere appropriate, from realms of fairy tale or science fiction fantasy to the more or less possible. They are encouraged to really imagine in detail doing some particular thing or things associated with this and to notice all sorts of details about the activity.

A storyteller is chosen and s/he has to explain what s/he is going to do or be and to also give as clear a picture as possible of how she will do the particular thing or things imagined. As in Fantastic Fibs, negative challenges ("That's impossible!" "You could never do that!" "It's really silly!" etc.) are completely forbidden. But also, the group or partner adopts the stance of being simply curious about how it is going to work rather than challenging and trying to prove that it won't. In addition to queries that can confirm details, questions can be asked about some of the mechanics of the fantasy ("How will you have learned to do that?" "How will you get the money to do that? etc) or about the consequences ("What sort of person will that make you?" "How will you cope with fame?" etc.).

The storyteller's turn is over either after a set number of questions (as in other games) or when the fantasy has obviously run its course and there are no new questions.

General Note: *This is a version of Tall Tale Telling that is future focused. It's essential to enforce the rule against negativity and ridicule and to emphasise the right kinds of questions, since personal fantasy can be a very sensitive area. It's normal and healthy to have dreams, especially as a child – even if they are not exactly realistic. (Indeed, one sign that a child might have a problem or two is a difficulty in imagining a positive future.) In developing the game, Pass it On can be used with the teller telling a tale about this person they know who is going to be x,y and z. Game 7 Hazards & Challenges can also be used to test the tale.*

Story Skills: *The game teaches controlled fantasy and the thinking through of a plot by experiencing it imaginatively. It also puts the storyteller in the middle of the story. Many writers have, of course, used their own future fantasies to create good fiction. The fantasy can be developed into a written piece either in the form worked out in the game or as a story about a heroine or hero who does this particular thing.*

Interesting: *A slight shift of emphasis, away from the story towards the tellers makes this a change instrument and a vehicle for moral teaching. Example morals to explore. 1. Everyone can have dreams and they don't need to be too realistic. 2. One can respect and even enjoy other people's fantasies. 3. Perspectives shared can be very interesting. 4. Imagination can be used to mobilise optimism, at the same time allowing people to conceive and realise the future.*

7.
HAZARDS & CHALLENGES

(Large or small groups or pairs or solo).

The storyteller has already created a fantasy of some kind, perhaps through one of the other tale games (or through writing part of a tale). For example, through Game 1. Fantastic Fibs s/he has suggested that s/he has a bike that flies, or through Game 17. Bragging, s/he claims to have a secret palace filled with many kinds of treasure. The fantasy is explained to the partner or group if necessary. S/he or they then have to introduce a series of hazards and challenges, chosen from a list which may include :-

★ physical dangers: the storyteller or her/his creation is threatened by this or that (real life) creature, thing or event.
★ fantasy dangers: the storyteller or her/his creation is threatened by this or that fantasy creature or thing or event
★ psychological dangers: being afraid or lonely or over-excited or angry etc.
★ difficult dilemmas etc. (keep the palace and lose the house?)
★ relationship difficulties (someone else might get hurt/offended/lost etc.)
★ temporary changes in the larger world (weather/war/mass celebrations etc.)
★ longer term changes in the larger world (land turns to desert/people decide not to value gold and treasure any more etc.)
★ any other kinds of challenge not fitting the categories above

Two or three categories of hazard/challenge are chosen to begin with and the storyteller can respond to two or three versions of each. The way the hazards and challenges are described will vary with age and understanding of the group. A developed game would include (at least) one of each kind of challenge. The storyteller describes how s/he copes with each hazard/challenge and may be allowed to 'reach base' – a destination or a goal which may be agreed in advance or improvised as the last hazard is dealt with.

General Note: An interesting way to handle the challenges in a group that requires some preparation is to make a pack of cards with challenges briefly described on each and have the storyteller pick (say) three cards. Children enjoy making the cards. Alternatively (in pairs or groups or alone) a list of six challenge types can be made and the storyteller throws a single dice a set number of times to pick the types to cope with.

Story Skills: This is a good way to develop a fantasy idea into a quest story or something similar. The link to writing may be fairly obvious. An additional advantage of the game is that it can teach the extended range of hazards and challenges, beyond obvious physical dangers, which in turn can make perception of what a story might be about a little more subtle.

Interesting: The game is rooted in optimism, which is powerful in itself. It is also develops conceptualisation of the range of challenges one may face in achieving something, rehearsing in fantasy ways of coping with them. And of course, as in other games, actual problems and challenges can be played out metaphorically with some groups and individuals.

8.
THE HOUSE THAT DAISY BUILT

Group Game

The idea is to invent something such as a house (or a car or a ship or whatever else) and to make it quite improbable and unlikely and even silly. In the example provided by the title, once the game has been explained, the leader might say: "The house that Daisy built was all made from candy." The next person might add: "Except for the doors, which were made from rope." Then the next person could add: "And the floors, which are made from sticky toffee." Someone else could add: "All the walls are covered with rubber." Which could be followed by: "and all the beds are made from apple pies." So it would go on.

When everyone has contributed, the whole thing can be replayed adding a few more details. The leader might say: "The purple house that the good Princess Daisy built was made from orange and yellow candy." The second would say something like: "Except for the two hundred doors, which were carefully woven from pink silk rope." And so on.

A further round (or more) can add extra detail, adjectives etc. to each person's contribution. Finally, group members are challenged to remember as much as possible of the whole 'story' of the house – though of course it's rare for anyone to recall more than a few of the details without practice. The one who can remember most is the winner.

The game can be repeated with other things made by other people.

———————————

General Note: This is a useful simple version of the well known story game, Story Chain in which everyone adds a little bit to a story in turn. It's fun to play and the images created can be marvellously bizarre and absurd. The techniques of replaying described can also be used with Story Chain. The game can also be played with small groups who can then swap their stories.

Story Skills: Another game which trains memory as well as invention. There are many things on which to focus – ways of describing, use of adjectives, use of exaggeration etc. The resulting picture can be used as a starting point in a game like Hazards & Challenges.

Interesting: The game is all about working together to invent something. As with some other games, the something that is to be invented can be more or less clearly a metaphor for something the players need to attain. For example, a house can obviously be community/team spirit/social balance etc. It's possible to use adaptations of the game as light-hearted ways of exploring solutions to current areas of concern.

9. THE ONE THAT GOT AWAY

Groups to pairs etc.

The fish that got away is always the biggest one, probably because there's still space left for imagining and exaggerating – like the Loch Ness Monster or the Yeti. Once something has been weighed and photographed and measured and cut up and labelled, there seems no mystery left. In this development of Fantastic Fibs, the teller invents a 'one that got away' yarn. This could be a phantom glimpsed somewhere, an incredible car or motorbike seen, a marvellous and magical jewel once found and since lost or a flying saucer or whatever.

To vary the procedure in the earlier game, the group can first experience their 'one that got away' through imagination. They can be asked to visualize and sense and touch and feel the stages of finding, registering mentally and then losing the thing etc. The storyteller is then chosen and has to explain in their telling of the tale:-

1. How was it seen, sensed, touched, smelt, heard etc. (i.e. a multi-sensory description should be encouraged).

2. How was it 'caught' and how did it 'get away'. (Or adaptations of these questions – a flying saucer might have been 'caught' on video; a jewel might have been 'caught' by buying a box at a jumble sale etc.)

3. Why is there now no record so that we have to trust the description? (The fish got away/the film or tape was wiped/ there was a hole in the sack etc.)

Questions are asked as in Fantastic Fibs. The game can be played in pairs and small groups as previously and extended through Pass it On.

General note: This development is more sophisticated because of the extra requirements – which need not all be enforced immediately. It is fairly easy to invent further variations of Tall Tale Telling games with more requirements as and when storytellers need stretching further.

Story Skills: This taps into what you could call an archetypal pattern in myth and legend. Imagining what might have been and what might be has created all kinds of things from dragons and giants to weird planets and utopias to answers to life, the universe and the meaning of everything. The extra demands on the storyteller naturally begin to impose a plot and give more discipline to the telling. For formal writing, the beginning-middle-end structure of the points make a useful frame for developing the tale.

Interesting: Questions of belief – exaggeration – trust in myth – separating fact from fantasy etc.

10.
A FUNNY THING HAPPENED

Groups to pairs etc.

This starts from the well known comedians' line. The funny (i.e. strange, bizarre, peculiar, odd, magical or whatever) thing that happened could be 'on the way here today' or it could have happened at some other time. It could have happened somewhere local everyone present probably knows, or in some other place entirely only known to the storyteller. It can be played as a first person game as in Fantastic Fibs or a third person game as in Wicked Whoppers. Before taking questions from the group or partner, the storyteller has to explain three things:-

1. Where the funny thing happened (describing the location well enough to give a picture).

2. What exactly happened (describing the strange happening as clearly as possible, how it was seen, whether other people were there etc.)

3. What it felt like (describing the storyteller's reactions or her/his central character's fear, joy, surprise etc.)

As an alternative to the more suspicious grilling of the basic Tall Tale Telling games, it can be explained that the group or partner can ask questions intended to be helpful. They can be persuading the storyteller to tell more of the tale or to suggest things s/he may not have thought of, things they themselves might like to have happened or imagine would be useful/interesting etc. (Younger children do this naturally in all of the games and usually need to be gradually schooled to ask more the more sceptical questions.) If this way of questioning is used, the storyteller has to work ideas suggested into the telling, rather than answering simply yes or no. A further variation is to ask a set number of questions at the end of each stage of the telling and to insist that these remain relevant to that stage, so that at the end of Stage 2, no questions are about Stage 1 etc.

General Note: *Another development of the basic Tall Tale Telling game using a three stage framework as in the previous game. This way of questioning can make the story grow quickly – with children working as a class or large group, it's best to recap on the story so far every so often so that extra elements can be remembered. This also develops memory and a feel for detail.*

Story Skill: *Further more disciplined storying, plus some hints of the way group stories (myths, legends etc.) develop as everyone makes a contribution. Points made in the notes to the previous game also apply. The game teaches incorporation of incidental detail and response to tangents.*

Interesting: *In one to one or small group work with children or adults who have had difficult experiences, it's possible to make the funny thing that happened fantastical and silly or strange or humourous, then to gradually hint at an underlying (safe enough) area of similarity to the troubling experiences, which has various healing possibilities.*

11.
PECULIAR PEOPLE

Small & large groups, pairs etc.

The storyteller has to invent a person from their family or street or town etc. who is peculiar in some way. S/he is extremely tall or small or has a head pointed like a pencil or has enormous hands – the unusualness can be pure fantasy or just within the bounds of the possible. Whatever makes her/him peculiar must be explained fully, giving a set number (between 3 & 7 depending on players' experience) of examples or consequences or effects of him/her being peculiar. (Very small woman – sometimes gets trodden on; doesn't need much food etc.) The partner or group then test the invention by asking questions and these must focus on how the peculiar person deals with up to seven further life circumstances (a lower number to begin with of course). The group sets up these one by one as obstacles for the teller, who responds immediately after each circumstance is described, showing how the peculiar person can always get over them, often using the peculiarity. The storyteller can (optionally) score a point for every obstacle successfully dealt with by using the peculiarity.

General Note: This is a development of Wicked Whoppers, the third person version of the basic tall tale telling game and combines an element of Game 7. Hazards & Challenges in the suggested second stage. It takes the basic game further, by introducing a limitation and, with Game 18 My Friend Boogle, illustrates ways further variations on the game might be developed. The story can be elaborated in Pass it On

Story Skills: The game suggests a story plot that is quite common. (Two songs from my CDs are useful for use with children here. My Fantastic Family *(from* The Wonderful Store *IJ101)* is just a list song about strange family members, whilst Vincent the Voice *(from* Wild Imaginings *IJ103 uses the full plot in a humourous setting.)* Stories coming out of the game can be written or may be developed further through oral work.

Interesting: Any peculiarity could have advantages (of course). Using wit and invention can make a disadvantage into an advantage. The game can be used with peculiarities which, whilst still in the range of the fantastic, might be analogous to actual concerns familiar to a group or individual.

12.
BEING JOE BLOGGS

(Large and small groups, pairs etc.)

In the basic game, the storyteller has to pretend to be a character in a particular story (e.g. in a fairy/wonder tale, the magician or the witch or the princess etc.) or a character type in stories in general (a giant or a dragon or a sorcerer, a crook or a bully etc.). The character can be from a well known story or from a tale made up in an earlier story game – or from a genre. S/he knows what it is like to be that character or character type. The group or partner ask her/him questions about what s/he did in the story or about the kinds of things s/he does in general. The storyteller can adopt mannerisms of the particular character/character type if they choose (i.e. speak like a witch or an ogre or a prince; present themselves as a gangster might etc.) The game can last as long as the character lasts or be restricted by number of questions.

In a more directly tall tale making variant of the game, the procedure is the same but the storyteller pretends to be someone else who did something extraordinary and impossible (the man who built a tower to the moon; the lady who kissed the tiger etc.) The person must not resemble the storyteller in any obvious way.

———————

General Note: Role playing games of this kind have been quite widely used. Although acting the role is fine, the focus of the game is really on telling the tale from a different point of view, hence it follows the pattern of other questioning games in this set. There are many ways to use the technique in the game differently and it is well worth experimenting.

Story skills: To write or tell a story, one needs a certain empathy with and understanding of the main characters, and those are skills and qualities practised in the game. Also, of course, telling a story in English from 'inside the skin' of a different person is at least as old as the works of Chaucer and is very much a recognised trick of the novelist.

Interesting: The technique can easily be adapted to allow participants to study from the inside the reactions and ideas of a person or character type they would not normally have any sympathy for. Part of human storying capacity seems to be the ability to imitate and go into role. It can be used to extend understanding and empathy as well as to problem solve.

13.
EXCELLENT EXCUSES

Large & small groups & pairs

The storyteller is asked for an excuse by the group or partner. Excuses asked for can range from the mundane and familiar, which make good places to start ("Why are you late?" "Why didn't you do x y z ...") to the possibly weird and peculiar ("Why did you wear that huge pink and purple suit at the weekend? " "How did you get that flying boat I saw you in?") The storyteller doesn't deny anything directly, but gives an excuse which should be as convoluted and fantastic as possible. ("I'm late because a dragon flew me all the way to France and then....." "I was in the flying boat because I forgot to let go of a firework and it took me to the moon and then I jumped off ..." A set number of curious and/or suspicious questions (say 5 or 7) can then be asked by the group and answered by the storyteller. At the end of the game, you can play back the excuse to give a long (and completely implausible) tall story.

General Note: The examples given suggest a game for primary age pupils, but this game can work well with any aged participants, with a little adaptation. There are various other ways of using excuse making creatively. For example, there can be an open season for excuses during one hour or day or week or other set period in the house or class or whatever. During that time, anyone who makes an imaginative and complicated enough excuse for some wrong action (or failure to take action) can get away with it (within agreed limits of course!). For young children, the classic picture book On the Way Home by Jill Murphy (Macmillan 1982) makes a perfect illustration of how this kind of tall tale can work.

Story Skills: Some people who claim to have neither imagination nor aptitude for stories can still make some extraordinary excuses. This is a great starting point for story making and keys participants into the logic of fiction – it has to add up to be even temporarily believable and we all should know this.

Interesting: Many people spend their lives making excuses in one way or another. Playing fantasy excuses is one way of working with this – within the protocols of this game, it's possible to slip in one or two themes which are near enough to the knuckle for a participant and yet, since you are playing a game, the tone can be kept light.

14.
RUM RUMOURS

(Small & large groups game)

The aim of this game is to invent the kind of rumour that is passed on as gossip or turns into an urban legend.

It involves three to five storytellers who claim to have witnessed something strange happening at one of a pre-set series of locations. (For example, public places such as theatres, supermarkets, churches, parks, beaches etc. – the list can be varied endlessly and can be discussed and agreed at the outset or simply given by a group leader.) The happening is to be within what participants might consider possible (which of course can go from just beyond the mundane all the way to the wacky wilds of UFOs and spooks, though again limits can be agreed). The group of storytellers have to tell the tale in turn, corroborating and extending each other's details, picking up and keeping in mind what has been said. They cook up the yarn together in discussions before sharing the tale.

As in *Fantastic Fibs*, they are asked questions by the larger group at the first (demonstration) stage, taking it in turns to answer. The groups can then swap yarns on the same pattern, the listening group making sure to ask each speaker at least three questions. The legend can then be developed in a version of *Pass it On* in which groups now take not the story they made up but the yarn they heard from the other group and tell it to another group. Stories can be passed on several times in this way. Each time, storytellers are free to make up bits they can't recall or freely elaborate bits which interest them. Whichever story a group heard last is retold to the larger group when it re-convenes. It is then compared with the yarn as told by the originators.

General Note: Several of the other games described as for solo tellers can be played in the manner of this game, or with pairs telling the tale. Obviously the tellers have to be encouraged to listen carefully to what has been said, whilst listeners are asked to spot flaws in the story logic or things that simply leave them curious to know more.

Story Skills: Stories of the kind that come out of this game are evolving around us all the time, In fact many newspapers are essentially involved in the process. Folk legends of some kinds have presumably been generated in this way, though of course attracting the sanction of tradition. Tellers in this game have to think quickly at the same time as listening. An interesting writing exercise is to then ask tellers to write the yarn they created without consulting each other and to later compare the stories for consistency etc.

Interesting: This is a great game for studying why things are believed, what might be rumour and supposition and so on. There are few people who have not been taken in by a legend or simply by misinformation at some stage in their lives.

15.
SMOKE WITHOUT FIRE

(Large and small groups; pairs)

There's no smoke without fire, runs the saying – though of course it's a very limited truth, because a lot of things might look like smoke and have nothing at all to do with fire.

The idea of this game is to jump to ridiculous and absurd conclusions, based on little bits of evidence. The storyteller leaves the room and the group agree to make, say, three facial expressions or action or gestures or signals. Or they might show three objects or scribbles or anything else that could be meaningful. The three 'signs' could be actually an attempt to communicate something ("Your shoe lace is undone." "There is a monster behind you." etc.) but they can also, as a variable, mean nothing at all. The storyteller, however, does not know this since the strategy is agreed whilst s/he is absent.

The storyteller returns and the group deliver the 'signs'. The storyteller has (say) three minutes (or more) to make as many wild and improbable guesses as possible. To score points, each guess must link together the signs into a brief narrative, rather than be explained separately as unconnected phenomena. They should be as ridiculous as possible – they may even score double points for silliness. The winner is the one who scores the most points of course. Once the game has been played as a large group game, it can be played in pairs, threes or small groups.

General Note: This makes a good party game and resembles charades. In a more formal context, limits can be set on permissible signs. In a school setting, it's rare for there to be time for more than two or three people to take the role with the large group. The brief stories can be elaborated further through games like Pass it On, Hazards & Challenges (and story elaborating games in Book 3).

Story Skills: The tendency to put two and two together and make five swans and a chimney sweep as it were is universal. It's basic to fiction making and this game resembles creative writing exercises which involve linking (say) three objects or pictures etc. Good fiction makers can turn anything into a story. The game develops the skill – and the bones of several stories are there for further development.

Interesting: The tendency described above is also at the root of some problems. Over imaginative linking of unconnected phenomena is seen in people who are excessively fearful, nervous, suspicious, jealous, malicious and all sorts more. The game is one way of studying this and also laughing at it and can be adapted to suit differing concerns.

16. SPRINGBOARDS

Pair game

This is a developed version of the basic Tall Tale Telling game in which the questioning and answering pattern is more strictly prescribed. It is for two players, though again can initially be played with the group and a volunteer storyteller. Player 1 (or the volunteer) is called IS and has to invent an apparently impossible thing s/he has seen, for example a tree a mile high. Player 2 (or the group) is called NOT and has to give one good reason why this could not be true (for example, if trees were a mile high, aeroplanes would bump into them). IS then has to use this objection as a springboard for her/his next idea (the tree is covered in lights like a huge Christmas tree) and NOT has to again advance a criticism or problem (if the tree is so big, how could they get all the lights in place and change the bulbs?).

As long as each player can do with s/he is supposed to ('spring' to further ideas (IS) and to criticise effectively (NOT)) the game can go on, though as in other games, it's useful to do a set number of 'moves' at the outset. Argument is strictly not allowed. When the game is over, IS has a kind of fantastic myth to recount and may like to make a note of this in some way (especially if *Pass it On* is to be played at the next stage), perhaps going back over the game with the partner or group so that answers can be recalled more easily or perhaps making written notes. In pairs, the game will then be played the other way around, IS becoming NOT and vice versa.

General Note: *Experience with basic tall tale telling games is assumed. Younger children may need some coaching before this game can be played smoothly. As implied, the story can be developed further if it is taken into a Pass it On game. The myth coming out of it can be thought of as complete in itself or can become part of a larger tale.* Hazards & Challenges (7) *is another game that can be used to follow this game.*

Story Skills: *Once participants can make up tales spontaneously through games like Fantastic Fibs, one needs to find ways to guide and discipline the fantasy. This game requires a step by step development of a basic fantastical idea, illustrating a principle that can be adapted to other styles of fiction, as well as to presentations of fact, design problems etc.*

Interesting: *This game calls for a degree of control. IS has to keep bouncing back and using an optimistic, problem solving approach. NOT has to keep referring back to the real world. Neither is allowed to quarrel as long as they are playing their parts properly. When it is familiar in a fantasy setting, the game structure can, like other games, be used in working with real life problems, which can (where appropriate) include emotional and relationship difficulties.*

17. BRAGGING

Trio game

This is a game for two players and a referee. A subject is picked by the referee, for example houses. The two players can spend a few moments thinking and imagining before starting, trying to see clearly their special house. Braggart A talks about a house that is particularly good in some way (it has a twenty rooms and each room has hundreds of things in it.)

Braggart A is allowed to say three things about the house to show that it is marvellous and special and very very good. Braggart B can ask one question about each of those three things to find out more and to test whether Braggart A has really 'seen' the house in question. S/he then says three things about a house that is even better. However, s/he is only allowed to go one better (one hundred and one rooms say) though the 'one' can be much exaggerated (that one room is bigger than all the others put together etc.). This goes on, with Braggart A adding some additional details of a different aspect of the house or whatever (it is painted with incredible paint every colour of the rainbow and you can see the colours a mile away). Again Braggart B has to go one better and so on.

Each player tries to remember everything he or she has said. It is the referee's job to monitor this in outline, perhaps making a brief note of each stage. The 'contest' can also be recorded on tape etc. At the end of an agreed number of moves or a set time limit, each braggart tells everything she or he has said again. The partner listens and can ask for an explanation of any inconsistencies or changes. S/he may then challenge what are felt to be inaccuracies. If the change doesn't square with what was said before, the challenger gets a point. If the change does square with what was said, the teller gets a point. The referee judges accuracy and his/her decisions are final. The winner is the one who completes his/her tale in recall and also scores the most points in the playback.

The referee can now be Braggart A, Braggart A becomes B and Braggart B becomes the referee. The game can be played three times, so that everyone has played each role once.

***General Note:** The full version of the game is a little complicated as described above, but works well with older children, teenagers and adults, obviously with some different suggestions as to content and direction. The principle of going one better can be adapted to make a simpler game in front of the group with younger children. The rule about accepting referees' decisions has to be enforced, even though referees will be fallible. Stories can be taken on to* Pass it On (2), Hazards & Challenges (7) *etc.*

***Story Skills:** The game intentionally develops both fantasy and memory. Each player has to find ways to remember what has been said. Usually players forget a lot to begin with as do referees. They should be encouraged to listen closely and make vivid mental images, as well as using their own brief note systems (letters, numbers, scribbles etc.), especially when playing the referee role. The myths created can be developed as written pieces.*

***Interesting:** The game illustrates how difficult it is to be consistent and to remember what one has said. By moving through the three different roles, players learn to be flexible, to take different stances, to stay alert and observe lying patterns.*

18.
MY FRIEND BOOGLE

Large & small groups; pairs

The storyteller talks about her/his (usually imaginary) friend who, though s/he might look ordinary, has this or that amazing and possibly fantastical skill or ability. (S/he can juggle with anything/ levitate/ run as fast as a car/ calculate any sum instantly/ turn purple/ disappear at will/ fly.) My Friend Boogle (the name changes for each player of course, which is part of the invention) is described briefly and her/his skill is detailed, with a graphic description of at least two minor occasions when the teller witnessed the skill. The group or partner ask three to seven practical questions to make details clear. The game can end at that point for novices and younger children.

With older/ more advanced players, the storyteller next relates a more dramatic incident during which the skill was put to the test. (S/he chased a bank robber/ rescued a child from a bully by turning purple/ flew over the crowds to take an important message.) The group or partner again ask questions to establish detail and the storyteller answers as he or she continues the narrative towards a successful outcome.

As the game becomes more familiar, partners and groups can put a set number of 'trials' into the story which the storyteller will have to cope with in the narrative. ("Don't forget that the bank robber has a gun." "The bully is always sick when he sees purple." "Amongst the crowd are duck hunters with bows and arrows who think the flying person is a duck.")

General Note: Like Peculiar People which it resembles, this is a development of Wicked Whoppers. The focus is on a skill and the onus is on the storyteller to supply the dramatic incidents that test and develop the invention. The final stage can be developed further by playing Game 7. Hazards & Challenges

Story skills: Particular skills lead to particular fictional possibilities. Even the classic cartoon super heroes only have particular sets of talents. In stories, the fiction can develop from exploring where a (very broadly defined) skill might take a person. Just about all developed fiction also tests the skill of central characters in one way or another.

Interesting: A skill is something you hone and develop; you are not born with it. This also applies to all kinds of life skills. The game can be used to test out particular life skills – confidence, resourcefulness, empathy etc. so that participants can clarify ideas about this, practising them in imagination.

19.
RAPID REVERSALS

Team game.

The group is split into two teams. One is called *Forwards* and the other is called *Backwards*. A story will be told around the group about a journey or a quest – or anything similar, though preferably something which will stand a little comedy. The basic 'territory' of the story can be mapped out and agreed in preliminary discussion or set by the leader, depending on the age and experience of the players.

The aim of the *Forwards* team is to get the central characters etc. forwards along the track towards whatever goal has been agreed, whilst the aim of *Backwards* is to rapidly reverse progress by offering a variety of hazards, banana skins, absurd circumstance, ridiculous coincidences etc. Team members usually contribute in turn to the tale.

A member of the Forwards team begins with a sentence or several establishing the 'forward momentum' and painting the central characters as good people. The *Backwards* team then counters with a bit of character assassination and their first reversal. They have two sentences for this. The reversal is supposed to be comic and silly, not tragic, so shouldn't be total disaster and destruction, unless a very zany version is preferred. (They take a wrong turning and end up back at home rather than a ten ton steam roller squashing them flat.)

All team members might be allowed to contribute once (or up to three times in a longer game) or the game can have a timed limit. *Forwards* aim with each contribution to right the wrongs set up by *Backwards* and to move the story further forwards toward the goal. They aim to reach it before whatever pre-set limit is reached and *Backwards* attempt to prevent this.

In an optional final stage for experienced participants, the invented story is retold, firstly by *Forwards*, who make the central characters heroes/heroines struggling against difficulties. *Backwards* follows, giving a different twist to the tale in which there are good reasons for stopping the heroes/heroines (they are impostors/ they are being saved from a trap/ there is an unconsidered danger in getting to the goal etc.)

A second game with a different scenario can follow in which *Backwards* becomes *Forwards* and *Forwards* becomes *Backwards*.

General Note: *This is a version of a well known story game in which one team is Good and the other is Evil (or something similar) and there is a comparable struggle to take the tale to a happy or an unhappy ending. It differs because Forwards is not necessarily the same as good, neither is Backwards evil; their roles can be more shaded. The optional replay at the end is also different. There are many ways to vary the protocols of this kind of game and these can be discovered through experiment.*

Story Skills: *Plots emerging from this game can be surprisingly sophisticated, especially when the Backwards team's take on things is explained. The replaying of the versions of the story can be handled as a written rather than an oral exercise in school literacy, adult creative writing etc. Making comparisons with the many quest tales from legend and literature can be interesting too.*

Interesting: *The game can be used to explore real life dilemmas in both public and private life, one side pushing for one outcome and the other for what appears to be its opposite. An interesting twist is to then play through the same scenario with teams taking the other side. In this setting, the tone still has to be kept light and humourous to avoid over-identification.*

20. CHALLENGING CHANGES

Large & small groups; pairs

"You wake up one morning and something has changed, something you normally take for granted..." The storyteller is given the challenge of describing a day when there has been a specific change, i.e. many and most things remain as previously, but there is one very important or obvious change. For example,

- ★ everything is suddenly a different colour
- ★ there is no colour at all, only black and white
- ★ all the animals are suddenly flying
- ★ people are walking backwards and vehicles are all in reverse
- ★ you have shrunk to the size of a mouse
- ★ you become extremely tall
- ★ you can understand what people are thinking

The change only lasts for a day. The game can be played in pairs or in groups. The storyteller does not choose the changes him/herself. In pairs, the partner sets the challenge. In a group, the leader either sets the challenge or chooses from suggestions made by the group. The storyteller has to say how s/he first noticed the change and some of the things that were different. She or he then takes one to three questions (as agreed in advance) and then tries to tell more of the yarn. If the players are inexperienced, questions can be asked in the same way as Fantastic Fibs and other basic games, i.e. about anything the partner or group need explaining to prove that the tale is true. If, however, the storyteller is able to tell the story without too much prompting, s/he can be stopped at the end of each sentence (or perhaps every three sentences) and asked questions about any of the detail. (If everyone was walking backwards, didn't they bump into each other?" "If you were tiny, why didn't your cat eat you?" etc.)

Questioning must be relevant to what has just been said and not revert to earlier statements or side issues.

The story ends as the day ends and a new day when things are back to normal begins. Playing back the story as told in the game gives a classic changes story.

General Note: A classic way of making a tall story or creating a fantasy world is simply to take the givens of everyday life and twist them a little – or a lot. As soon as everything has changed colour or size or shape, you have a different world, as very many writers and other fiction makers have discovered.

Story Skills: Restricting the change to one element or factor is good discipline and shows how a fantasy world can be created by simply changing one or two normal expectations. In oral telling, the fantasy changes are usually sketched briefly, often using the Rule of Three or different kinds of list technique (see Book 3, Patterns on the String *for further explanation, games etc.), allowing attention of the audience to be maintained. Written telling sometimes allows more scope for exploring detail, a point worth elaborating in sessions. The instruction in this game also makes a good creative writing exercise. Indeed, it's possible to write a tale first and then play the oral game using the remembered text.*

Interesting: A version in the game can be played with individuals and groups for directly therapeutic purposes. The set change removes a source of difficulty for the individual or group (having no confidence/ being unfocused/ being unhappy etc.) and the storytellers have to create a story of what they do in the one day without the 'problem'. In the process, they rehearse actually doing without a problem, which can be very empowering.

21.
TIME CHANGES

Large & small groups; pairs

"You are given five time skills. You are able to step forwards in time and backwards in time. You can make time go quickly and slowly and you can also stop time. But you can only do each of these things once, though after each time change you can return to ordinary time so that you are not stuck."

This is the (approximate) preliminary instruction given to the storyteller, who has to tell the beginning of a yarn explaining how s/he received this special, limited skill of using time and what s/he decided to try to achieve by using it (winning fame or fortune; getting money; rescuing someone; helping people; discovering a secret etc.) and how s/he began her or his quest.

The group or partner now invents a danger or hazard or difficulty for him or her to overcome and s/he uses one of the skills to overcome it and continue with the tale. The group or partner introduces another danger etc. and the storyteller uses another time change to deal with it and so on through five hazards to match the five time skills. When all five skills have been used to conquer five dangers, the storyteller may be near or far from the goal and has a chance to make the final 'leap' successfully with no hazards. To make this stage difficult, s/he may only use one extra sentence to do this, though this rule can be left out at the initial stage.

General Note: Related to Challenging Changes of course, this game incorporates some of Hazards & Challenges too, with the limitation that hazards are dealt with in one way. Specifying the use of particular categories of hazard and challenge as in that game is useful in this one.

Story skills: Whilst this can be a game for inventing science fiction plots, playing tricks with time is part of much fiction making, since one is very often skating over these events, emphasising those etc. Skill in handling time is practised in the game, along with adroit and flexible creative thinking.

Interesting: It's common for people not only to spend but actually to squander time, often simultaneously complaining about their lack of it. The game can, for an appropriate player, provide a way of looking at this, especially if the challenges are in the realms of the psychological or moral.

22.
I WENT TO THE PICTURES TOMORROW

Pairs & trios with larger groups sharing

This is a language game, based on a rhyme I learned in primary school which begins:-

I went to the pictures tomorrow
And had a front seat at the back
An old lady gave me an apple
I ate it and gave it her back....

The aim of the full game is to make a story which consists of a series of impossible, paradoxical statements, as in the rhyme. The idea can be explained to a group through the lines of the rhyme and experiments can be made in inventing single sentences that work in similar ways. (I will go to the seaside yesterday.... I sat in the boot beside the driver... A young man gave me his pension book, so I burned it, then read it out loud... etc.)

Once the idea is explained, pairs or trios can be sent away to make up a series of impossible statements together through discussion. They could memorise each phrase or record them in writing. These don't have to be linked initially – the group can convene again and share impossibles, challenging any that don't fit the pattern. They can then return to pairs or work alone to link a series of statements to make a longer 'story' of impossibles. (The lines don't have to scan as in the rhyme.)

This is then recited and the pair with the most impossibles wins. However, the group can challenge any line that is not impossible.

General Note: The full version of this game is difficult for younger children of course, though some can grasp the early stages described above quite easily. More or less the full game can be made to work with individual children as young as five or six with the right kind of adaptation. For older children, teenagers and adults, this kind of word created tall tale is a useful contrast to styles coming out of other games and can be integrated into presentation structures such as Magic Island & Strange Planets (23) News for the Emperor (24).

Story Skills: As a purely oral game, this trains memory as well as invention. Both written and oral versions make interesting ways of looking at grammar without being too technical. Creating nonsense in this way, incidentally, has a very long history in both oral and literary tradition.

Interesting: This is a good exercise for people of all ages are inclined to try too hard to be clever and conversely, for those who are daunted by the sound of the apparently clever. It's a light-hearted way of showing that just because you can say something, it doesn't mean that it automatically makes sense.

23.
MAGIC ISLANDS & STRANGE PLANETS

(Pairs, small and large groups, solo work;
also presentation framework)

The storyteller pretends s/he has visited a magic island or strange planet. S/he has to explain how s/he got there, describe what makes the place magic or strange and give details of at least three things s/he saw. S/he should say, too, how s/he got back again. When it all happened and whether anyone else was involved might also be part of the basic brief, or may be left to come out in the questioning.

Extra points are scored for adventures on the island/planet. The group or partner question him/her about things/colours/strange sights seen, noises heard, scents scented, feelings felt etc., roughly how s/he survived it all, practicalities of the journey, things if any brought back, how, why and if it was all kept a secret and so on.

As a variant, the storyteller might be asked to tell a tale involving not just one but three or more islands or planets, with some information about how he or she travelled between places.

The game structure leaves a fantasy adventure or quest story, which can then be told in full.

General Note: There is a famous Irish story, The Voyage of Mael Dun, which is included in some books of Celtic lore (e.g. Myths & Legends of the Celtic Race – *T.W.Rolleston Constable 1985*) and is originally from a bardic recitation recorded in the Book of the Dun Cow *(circa 1100)*. Mael Dun (pronounced Muldoon) and his men, on a quest to find the killer of the hero's father and cursed with bad luck, travel from island to island witnessing all kinds of strange wonders. The story makes an excellent template for this game and many of the wonders (suitably edited) fascinate children – islands of golden apples and fiery pigs, islands of giant horses, magic fountains etc. (We plan to publish a summary in the Resources section of the Imaginary Journeys web site shortly.)

Story Skills: In schools or in group workshops, a large or small group telling can be developed for presentation to other groups (or with children, in an assembly), with islands taken from different individual tales and incorporated into a longer narrative, telling how the journey of all the tellers began, how they moved from island to island and how they got back again. Alternatively, individual written developments can follow the quest structure suggested by the game with any suitable variations and diversions. The fantasy islands can bring together different kinds of fantasy developed in other games (such as Games 20 Challenging Changes, 21. Time Changes or 22. I Went to the Pictures Tomorrow) and give an exercise in controlling and using these.

Interesting: Working together with imagination; compromising to make a group tale; creating ideal imaginary worlds; opening up minds to varieties of fantasy etc.

24.
NEWS FOR THE EMPEROR

Group game; also presentation framework

This group game is for experienced tall tale tellers and draws some of the telling skills together in a framework, perhaps for a performance or presentation. It is based on a Chinese folktale in which the Emperor has announced that he will give his daughter in marriage to any man who can give him news that is so odd or marvellous and strange that he will be surprised and say that it's real news to him – or simply that it's a lie. As princes and storytellers of all kinds come with their fantastic yarns, the excited courtiers ask them curious questions about each strange account. The emperor, however, simply yawns at all the talk of marvellous mountains and enormous apes and drums the size of palaces and says that he knows all about them already....

The scenario is explained and the group must, one by one, give news to the Emperor of something so strange and peculiar and odd that he (or she) will be surprised. The group leader can play the part of the Emperor (or, with children, can choose an Emperor from the group).

Played as a game, this works best when no one has heard the tale – or any of the many variants on this pattern from around the world in which someone has to make someone else call him or her a liar. If any group members know the plot, they are told to hold back their knowledge of how the Emperor could be tricked and simply offer something strange and fantastic when it's their turn.

Each marvel can be noted down or memorised as it is told. The group, playing the part of the courtiers, can ask say three questions about each marvel (if there is time), so that each group member's 'story' can grow a little. Finally, when everyone has had a turn, the last part of the story is told.

After many tales had been told to the Emperor, a young man came with seven friends, each carrying baskets, and demanded repayment. His father, he claimed, had loaned the emperor seven baskets of gold many years before and that is why the Emperor is rich whilst his father is poor. The Emperor automatically denies it, says he doesn't believe it, that it's a lie. And so the young man marries the princess.

The tale can now be replayed as a group telling, initially with all of the fantastic yarns included – though, to avoid losing the audience if it is retold in front of others, some editing and selecting may be required.

General Note: The denouement in some of the many other folktales mentioned above has a King (or similar figure) affronted and taken by surprise by an accusation that his father and mother were thieves or cheats and/or that he is a bastard/impostor or is known for his ugliness/meanness etc. and so on. This may appeal more to some older groups and can be substituted. (e.g. The King of Liars – p.424 A Dictionary of British Folktales Part A – Katharine Briggs, Routledge 1970)

Story Skills: A presentation makes a good excuse to edit and refine down some of the stories, make judgements on what works, get storytellers to be relevant, focused etc. The kind of tall tale telling demanded will already have been developed through other games in the book. Again, transition from oral to written work should be fairly clear. (For ways to develop the storytelling in the framework, see Book 3 Patterns on the String.)

Interesting: The tale throws up some good questions about why people believe things. Also what it is that makes people forget judgements and jump into automatic action.

Imaginary Journeys is about using imagination in all sorts of ways. Please visit our web site to discover more about the range of products and services we are developing, both creative and therapeutic or to find free downloads of song lyrics, notes, information, writings on storytelling etc.

We also welcome any feedback on publications and audio products. Please write or e-mail:

Imaginary Journeys,
27 London Road,
Tonbridge,
Kent TN10 3AB
Tel/fax+44 (0) 1732 362356

Web site: www.imaginaryjourneys.co.uk
E-mail: info@imaginaryjourneys.co.uk

END PIECES

Tall Stories

My house is made of sugar
With a roof of coconut ice,
The stairs are made from nougat
In the walls live chocolate mice.
You can eat it all,
There's a humbug hall,
Every room has a liquorice door.
When I've no bread,
I eat my bed,
And sleep on the marshmallow floor!

from 'Tall Stories' by Rob Parkinson, a fantasy song recorded on The Wonderful Store CD/cassette (see inside back cover)

Winston & the Wolves

Winston heard the wolves in the kitchen one night
When his mum & dad were fast asleep.
Their barks and their howls woke him up in a fright
And made his flesh start to creep.
But he plucked up his courage and he walked downstairs
It made him angry to think of them there.
And there they were with red eyes all big:
Six wild wolves stealing goodies from the fridge!

Wolves can be wicked, wolves can be wild
But wild wicked Winston had the wolf-taming style.

From Winston & the Wolves, a fantasy narrative song by Rob Parkinson, recorded on Wild Imaginings CD (see inside back cover).

The Lying Minister

Long and long ago, a certain Queen decided that no one should tell lies in her city.

This seemed a very good idea to begin with, but very quickly everyone realised how difficult it was to live without lies. You couldn't tell people they looked well unless they really did, you couldn't flatter anyone to give them confidence, you couldn't say all sorts of things in ordinary conversation without worrying that you might be reported to the queen's spies and hauled off to gaol. And you certainly could not tell stories. Fiction of all kinds was strictly banned.

Because of all that, everyone started to be unhappy and that led to people being unable to do their work as well as they could. Fun became a distant memory. Something had to be done. The queen, however, stuck to her guns and all the clever philosophers and thinkers at the court supported her. Lying was wrong.

There was, however, one honest minister who had formerly been known as a bit a of a teller of tales. One day, he says to the queen: "If I can show you the foolishness of the bind you have put on your people, will you then let me tell you a story?."

Though she was furious at this remark, the queen agreed and the minister announced before all the court: " I am an honest man and I tell you all that this day before midnight, I shall have told a blatant lie. Watch me well." The minister then sat still, in absolute silence until midnight.

Well, he'd proved his point and the queen recognised the fact. So she abandoned her law and let him tell a story and he made it as true as he could . But as for that story, I can't tell it to you now so you'll have to imagine it for yourself.